essential
Musicianship
for band

INTERMEDIATE

ensemble
concepts

Eddie Green

John Benzer

David Bertman

Percussion by
Evelio Villarreal

ISBN 978-0-634-09483-5

HAL•LEONARD®
CORPORATION
7777 W. BLUEMOUND RD. P.O. BOX 13819 MILWAUKEE, WI 53213

Welcome to . . .

Welcome to *Essential Musicianship for Band* and *Ensemble Concepts – Intermediate Level.*

Ensemble Concepts is designed to help you and your fellow band members learn more about playing in an ensemble. While learning the basics of playing your own instruments, these exercises will help your entire band or ensemble understand the important steps to making a rich, musical sound as a group.

As you play and learn from *Ensemble Concepts*, it's important to:

 LISTEN carefully to your own
sounds and to those around you.

 FOLLOW your director's suggestions as you
work on the goals listed with each exercise.

 STRIVE to do your part to improve the
sound of the entire band or ensemble.

 REMEMBER that a good musical group is the result
of all its players working together like a team.

 ENJOY the great sounds that come from a music
group that likes to learn and perform together.

The skills learned in *Ensemble Concepts* will prepare you and your ensemble for all the great music that awaits you. As you progress, you'll be amazed how enjoyable and rewarding playing an instrument in a group can be, whether it's band, orchestra, or just a small group with friends.

Good luck and have fun with all your music experiences!

1. Ensemble Sound

1-1 Block Concert F

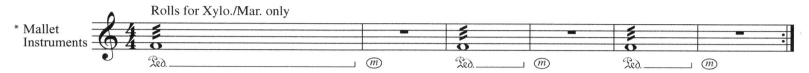

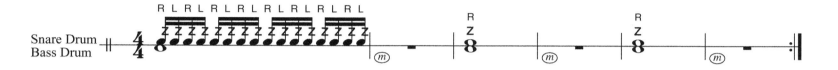

 = Muffle (dampen)
*Xylophone, Bells, Marimba, Vibes
Ped. (Vibes only)

Percussion Goals
1. Breathe together.
2. Start together.
3. Strike the instrument in the same place with the same energy every time.
4. All strokes should have a smooth beginning, middle and end.
5. Match the dynamic level of the wind players.

1-2 Matching Sections – Non-Touching Notes

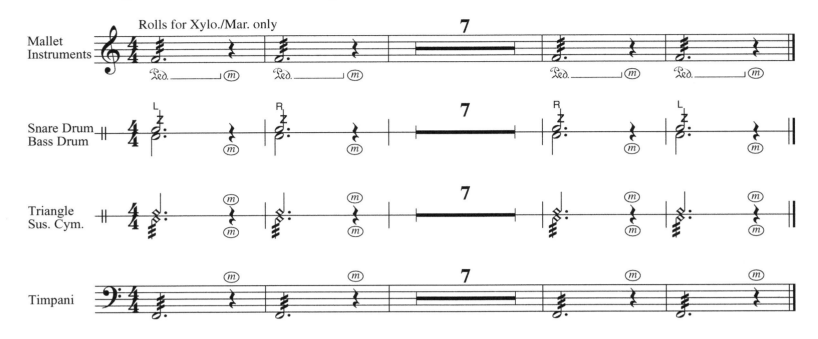

 Percussion Goals
1. Breathe together.
2. Start together.
3. Strike the instrument in the same place with the same energy every time.
4. All strokes should have a smooth beginning, middle and end.
5. Match the dynamic level of the wind players.

1-3 Matching Sections – Touching Notes

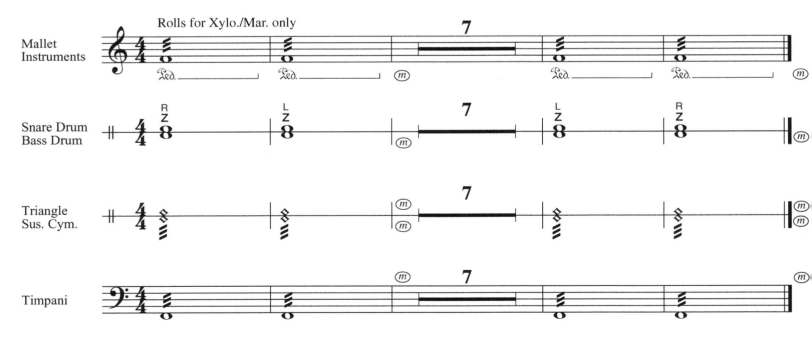

 Percussion Goals
1. Breathe together.
2. Start together.
3. Strike the instrument in the same place with the same energy every time.
4. All strokes should have a smooth beginning, middle and end.
5. Rolls should be smooth and even.

2. Rhythm and Tonguing Exercises

2-1 Long to Short Notes

ⓜ = Muffle (dampen)
*Xylophone, Bells, Marimba, Vibes
🎵 Ped. (Vibes only)

Percussion Goals
1. Breathe together.
2. Start together.
3. Strike the instrument in the same place with the same energy every time.
4. The quicker the notes, the smoother the mallet/stick motion should look.
5. Rolls should be smooth and even.

2-2 Short to Long Notes

Percussion Goals
1. Breathe together.
2. Start together.
3. Strike the instrument in the same place with the same energy every time.
4. The quicker the notes, the smoother the mallet/stick motion should look.
5. Rolls should be smooth and even.

2-3 Long to Short Notes

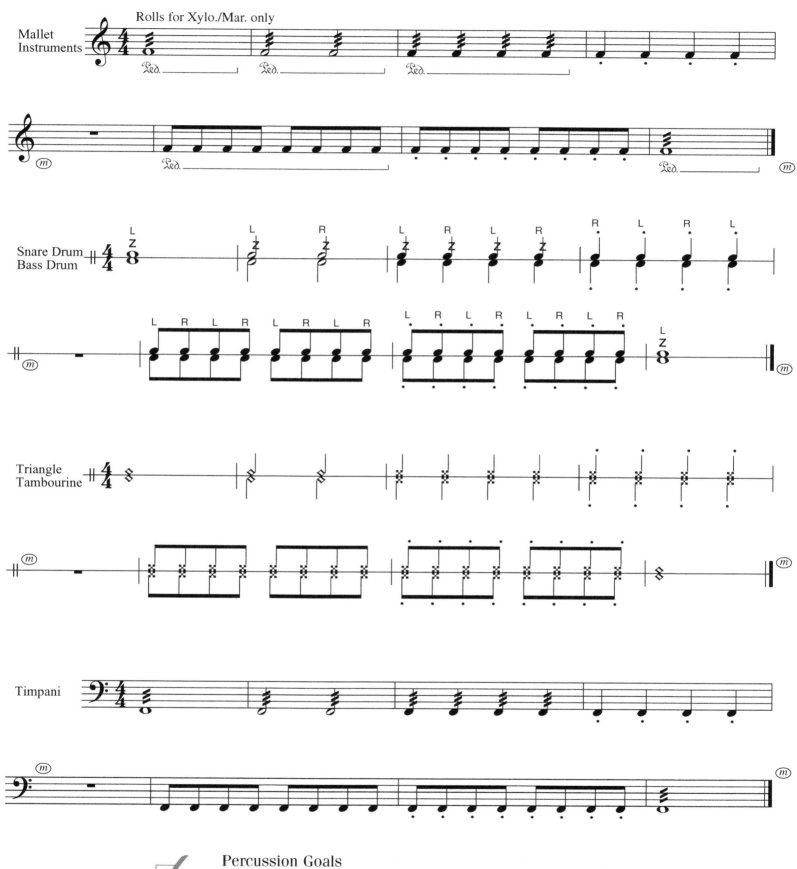

Percussion Goals
1. Breathe together.
2. Start together.
3. Strike the instrument in the same place with the same energy every time.
4. The quicker the notes, the smoother the mallet/stick motion should look.
5. Rolls should be smooth and even.

2-4 Long to Short Notes

2-5 Short to Long Notes

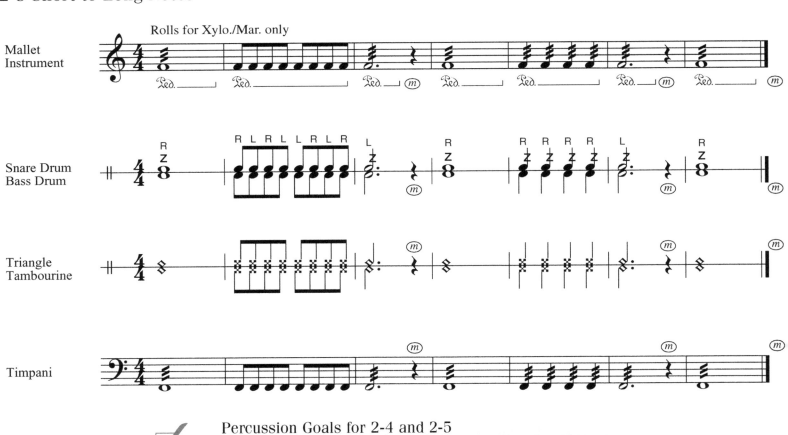

Percussion Goals for 2-4 and 2-5

1. Breathe together.
2. Start together.
3. Strike the instrument in the same place with the same energy every time.
4. The quicker the notes, the smoother the mallet/stick motion should look.
5. Rolls should be smooth and even.

3. Intervals Moving Down and Up

3-1 Intervals Down

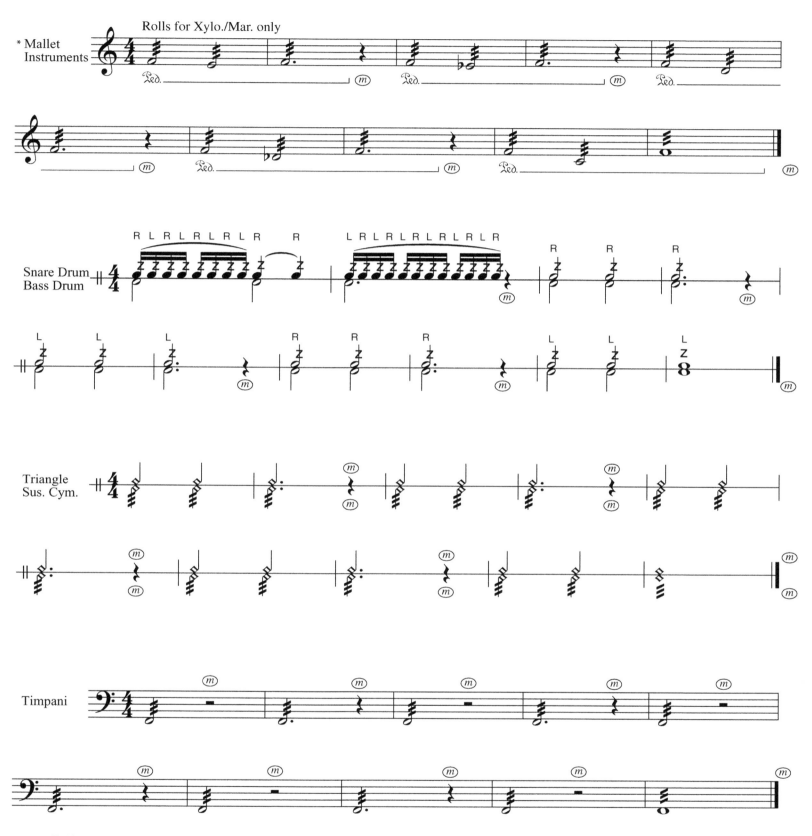

 = Muffle (dampen)
*Xylophone, Bells, Marimba, Vibes
Ped. (Vibes only)

Percussion Goals

1. Breathe together.
2. Posture should be natural with the body position balanced.
3. Strike the instrument in the same place with the same energy every time.
4. Match the dynamic level of the winds.
5. Rolls should be smooth and even.

3-2 Intervals Up

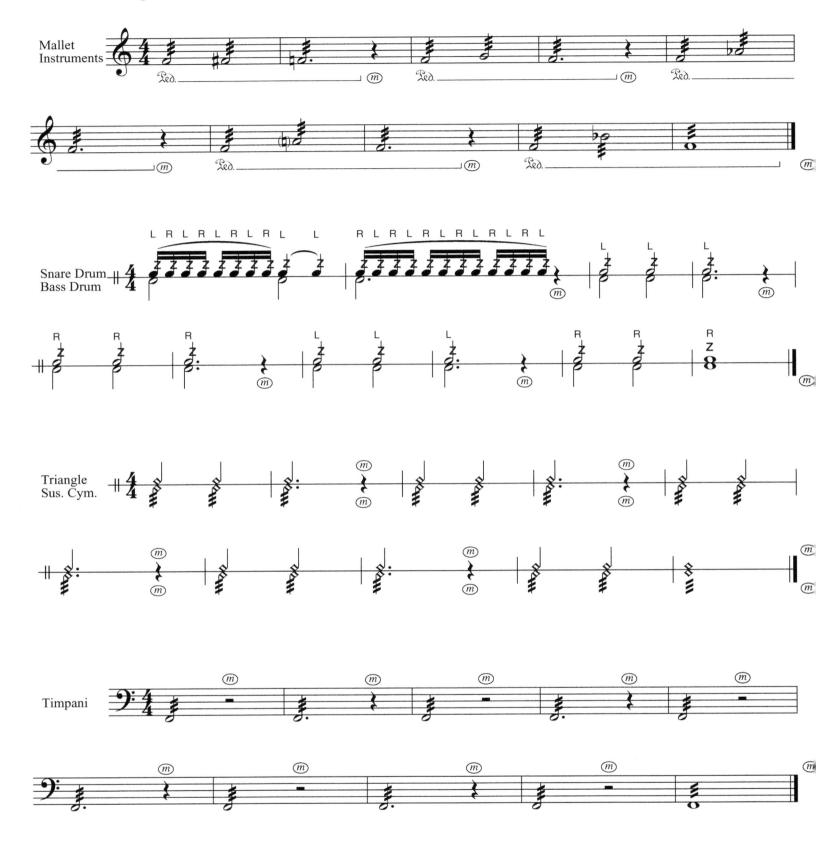

Percussion Goals

1. Breathe together.
2. Posture should be natural with the body position balanced.
3. Strike the instrument in the same place with the same energy every time.
4. Match the dynamic level of the winds.
5. Rolls should be smooth and even.

3-3 Intervals Up and Down

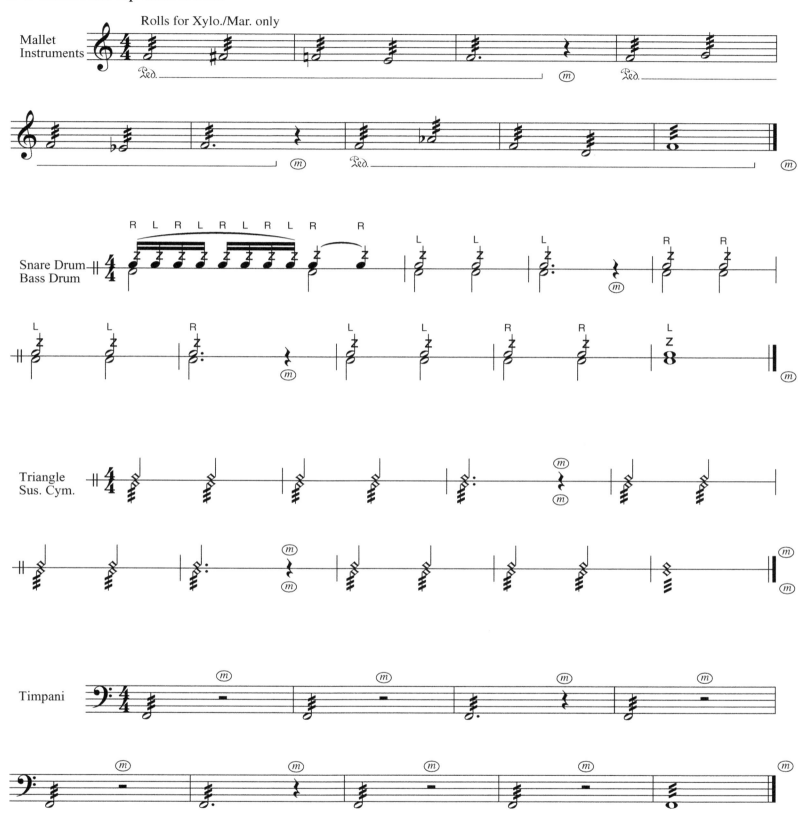

Percussion Goals
1. Breathe together.
2. Posture should be natural with the body position balanced.
3. Strike the instrument in the same place with the same energy every time.
4. Match the dynamic level of the winds.
5. Rolls should be smooth and even.

3-4 Intervals Up and Down (Model and Ensemble)

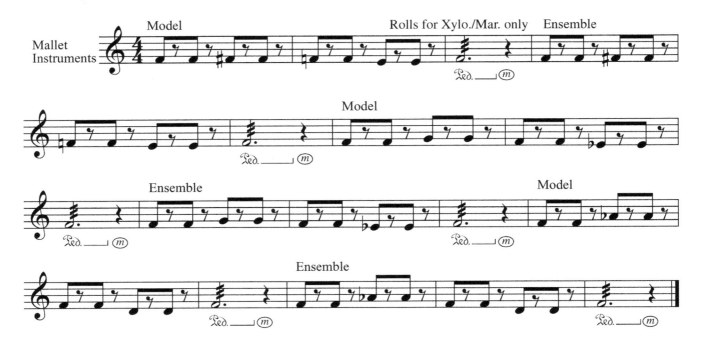

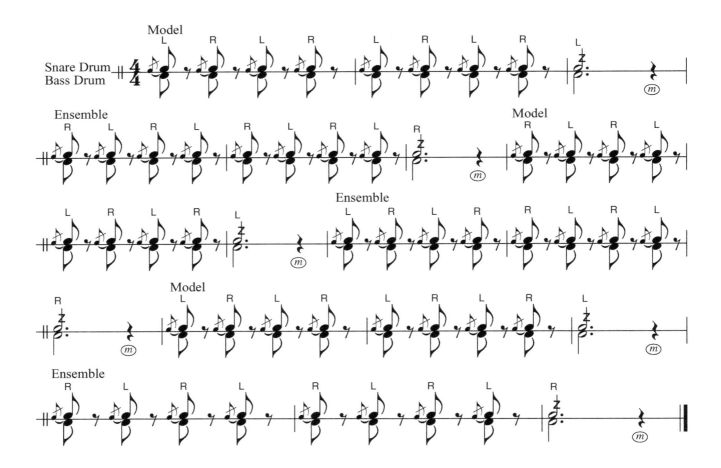

3-4 Intervals Up and Down (cont.)

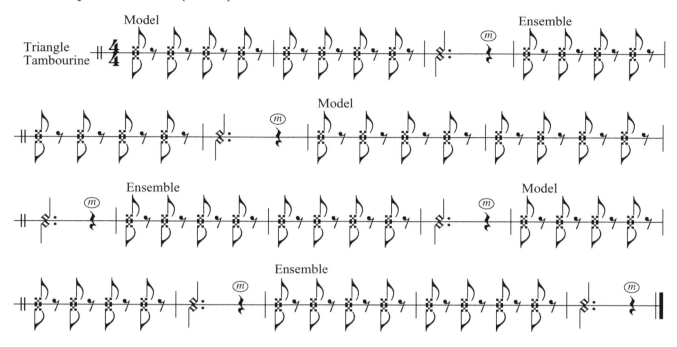

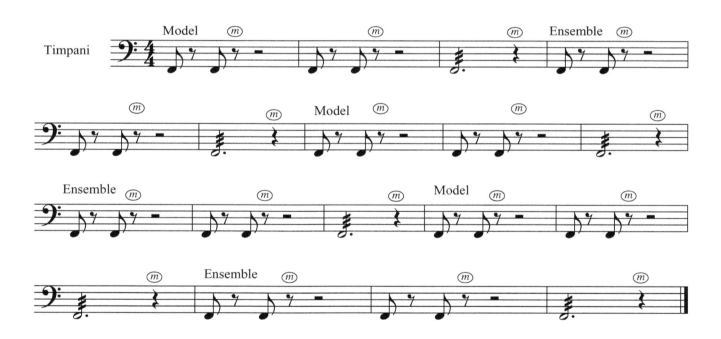

 Percussion Goals

1. Breathe together.
2. Posture should be natural with the body position balanced.
3. Strike the instrument in the same place with the same energy every time.
4. Match the dynamic level of the winds.
5. Rolls should be smooth and even.

4. Pick-up Exercises

4-1 Moving Up

* Mallet Instruments

Snare Drum
Bass Drum
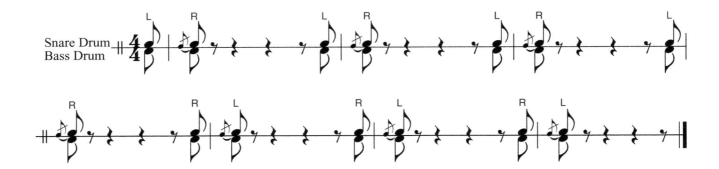

Triangle
Tambourine
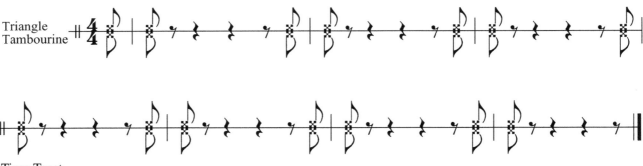

Timp. Tacet

 = Muffle (dampen)
*Xylophone, Bells, Marimba, Vibes
℘. (Vibes only)

Percussion Goals
1. Breathe together and start together.
2. Each pick-up note should strengthen to beat 1 (downbeat).
3. The quicker the notes, the smoother the mallet/stick motion should look.
4. Match the dynamic level of the winds.
5. Hands, wrists and arms should look natural and feel soft and relaxed.

4-2 Moving Up (2 notes)

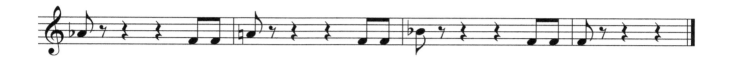

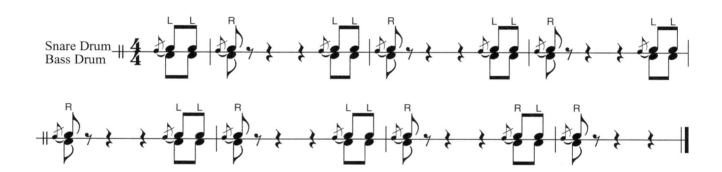

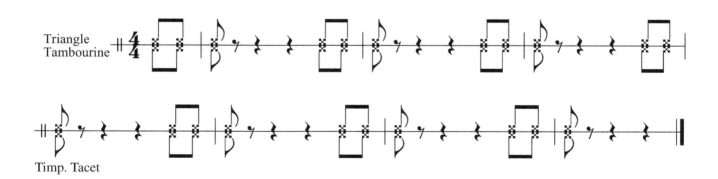

Timp. Tacet

Percussion Goals

1. Breathe together and start together.
2. Each pick-up note should strengthen to beat 1 (downbeat).
3. The quicker the notes, the smoother the mallet/stick motion should look.
4. Match the dynamic level of the winds.
5. Hands, wrists and arms should look natural and feel soft and relaxed.

4-3 Moving Up (3 notes)

Mallet Instruments

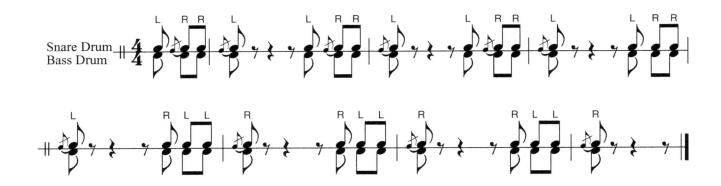

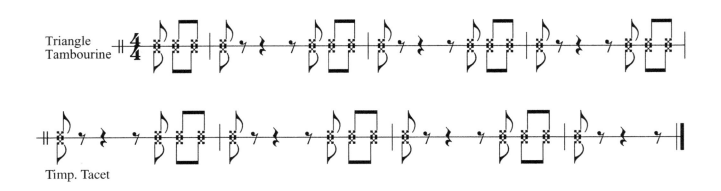

Snare Drum
Bass Drum

Triangle
Tambourine

Timp. Tacet

Percussion Goals

1. Breathe together and start together.
2. Each pick-up note should strengthen to beat 1 (downbeat).
3. The quicker the notes, the smoother the mallet/stick motion should look.
4. Match the dynamic level of the winds.
5. Hands, wrists and arms should look natural and feel soft and relaxed.

4-4 Moving Down

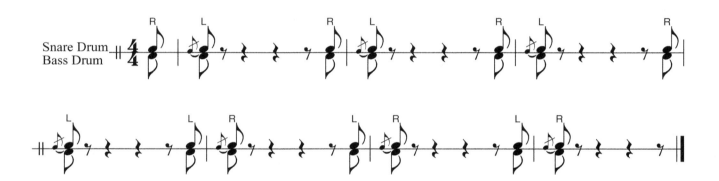

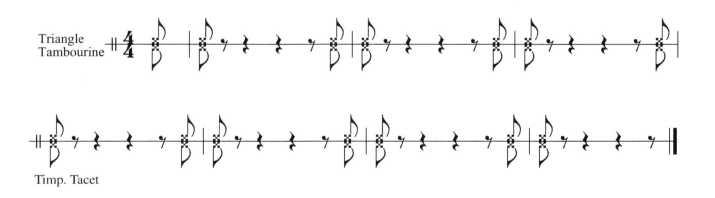

Timp. Tacet

 Percussion Goals
1. Breathe together and start together.
2. Each pick-up note should strengthen to beat 1 (downbeat).
3. The quicker the notes, the smoother the mallet/stick motion should look.
4. Match the dynamic level of the winds.
5. Hands, wrists and arms should look natural and feel soft and relaxed.

4-5 Moving Down (2 notes)

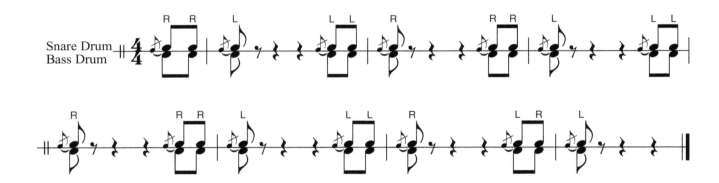

Timp. Tacet

 Percussion Goals
1. Breathe together and start together.
2. Each pick-up note should strengthen to beat 1 (downbeat).
3. The quicker the notes, the smoother the mallet/stick motion should look.
4. Match the dynamic level of the winds.
5. Hands, wrists and arms should look natural and feel soft and relaxed.

4-6 Moving Down (3 notes)

Mallet Instruments

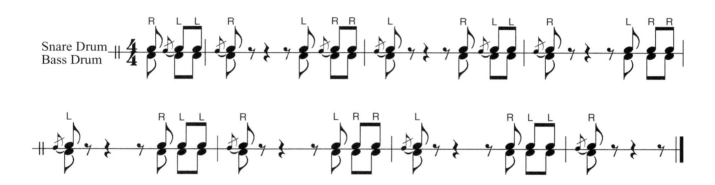

Snare Drum
Bass Drum

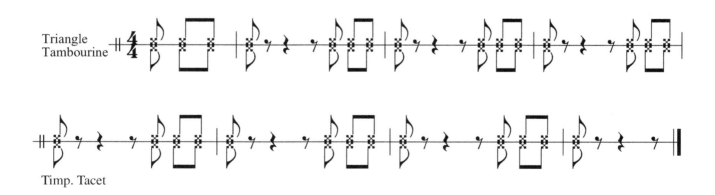

Triangle
Tambourine

Timp. Tacet

Percussion Goals
1. Breathe together and start together.
2. Each pick-up note should strengthen to beat 1 (downbeat).
3. The quicker the notes, the smoother the mallet/stick motion should look.
4. Match the dynamic level of the winds.
5. Hands, wrists and arms should look natural and feel soft and relaxed.

5. Learning a Major Scale

Step 1 — *Mallet Instruments, Snare Drum / Bass Drum, Triangle / Tambourine, Timpani

Step 2 — Mallet Instruments, S.D. / B.D., Triangle / Tambourine, Timpani

Step 3 — Mallet Instruments, Snare Drum / Bass Drum, Triangle / Tambourine, Timpani

Percussion Goals for Steps 1-3

1. Breathe together and start together.
2. Strike the instrument in the same place with the same energy every time.
3. Posture should be natural with the body position balanced.
4. Return the mallets/sticks to their starting position during rests and at the end of the exercise.
5. Hands, wrists and arms should look natural and feel soft and relaxed.

m = Muffle (dampen)
*Xylophone, Bells, Marimba, Vibes
Ped. (Vibes only)

 Percussion Goals for Steps 4-5

1. Breathe together and start together.
2. Strike the instrument in the same place with the same energy every time.
3. Posture should be natural with the body position balanced.
4. Return the mallets/sticks to their starting position during rests and at the end of the exercise.
5. Hands, wrists and arms should look natural and feel soft and relaxed.

6. Major Scale Exercises

6-1 Moving Down and Up (Tonguing and Slurring)

*Mallet Instruments

Snare Drum
Bass Drum

Triangle
Tambourine
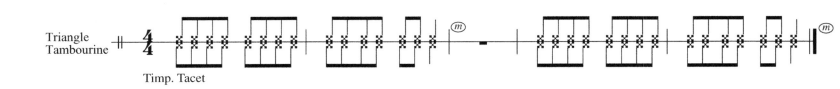

Timp. Tacet

6-2 Moving Up and Down (Tonguing and Slurring)

Mallet Instruments

Snare Drum
Bass Drum

Triangle
Tambourine
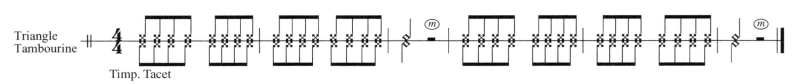

Timp. Tacet

ⓜ = Muffle (dampen)
*Xylophone, Bells, Marimba, Vibes
Ped. (Vibes only)

Percussion Goals for 6-1 and 6-2
1. Breathe together and start together.
2. Strike the instrument in the same place with the same energy every time.
3. The quicker the notes, the smoother the mallet/stick motion should look.
4. Rolls should be smooth and even.
5. All flams should have the same quality of sound.

7. Learning a Chromatic Scale

7-1 Moving Up (6/8)

Step 1

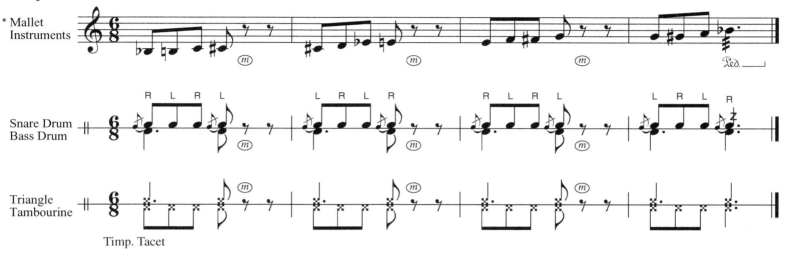

Timp. Tacet

Step 2

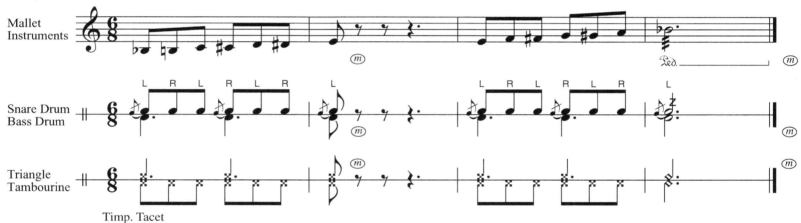

Timp. Tacet

Step 3

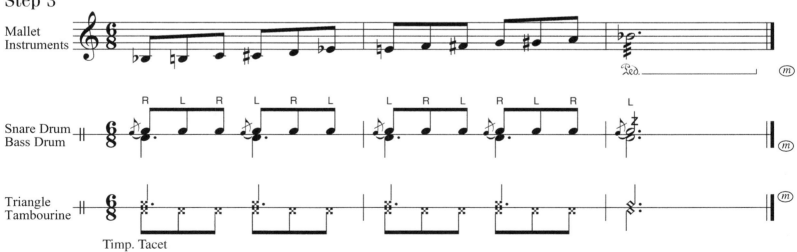

Timp. Tacet

 = Muffle (dampen)

*Xylophone, Bells, Marimba, Vibes

Ped. (Vibes only)

Percussion Goals for 7-1 (all steps)
1. Breathe together and start together.
2. Strike the instrument in the same place with the same energy every time.
3. Stroke beginnings should be smooth.
4. Hands, wrists and arms should look natural and feel soft and relaxed.
5. All flams should have the same quality of sound.

7-2 Moving Down

Step 1

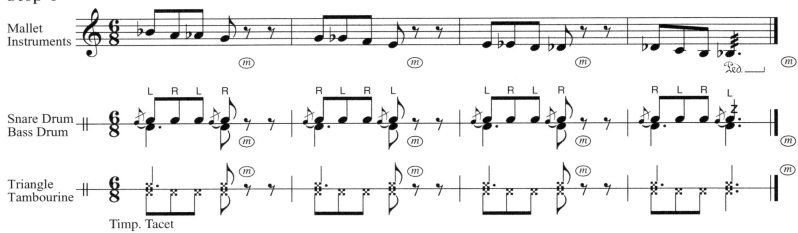

Mallet Instruments

Snare Drum
Bass Drum

Triangle
Tambourine

Timp. Tacet

Step 2

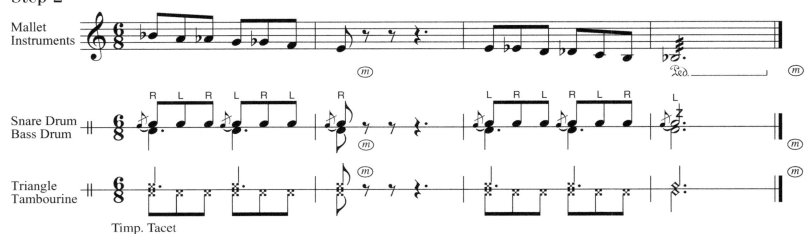

Mallet Instruments

Snare Drum
Bass Drum

Triangle
Tambourine

Timp. Tacet

Step 3

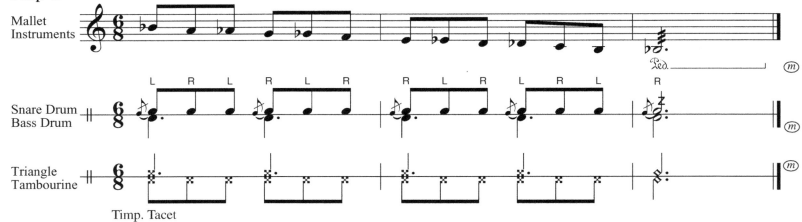

Mallet Instruments

Snare Drum
Bass Drum

Triangle
Tambourine

Timp. Tacet

Percussion Goals for 7-2 (all steps)

1. Breathe together and start together.
2. Strike the instrument in the same place with the same energy every time.
3. Stroke beginnings should be smooth.
4. Hands, wrists and arms should look natural and feel soft and relaxed.
5. All flams should have the same quality of sound.

7-3 Moving Up (4/4)

Step 1

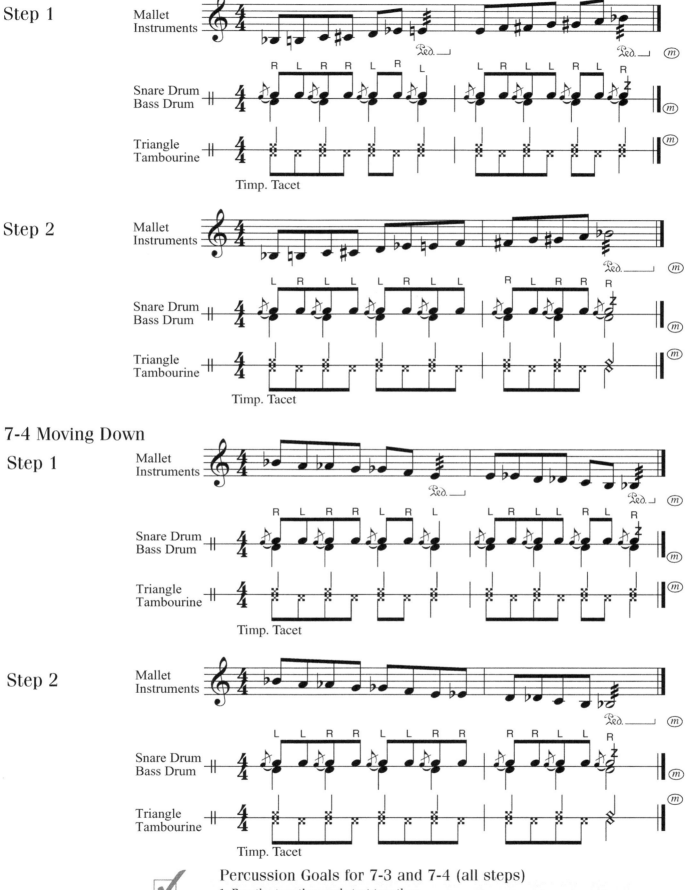

7-4 Moving Down

Step 1

Step 2

Percussion Goals for 7-3 and 7-4 (all steps)

1. Breathe together and start together.
2. Strike the instrument in the same place with the same energy every time.
3. Stroke beginnings should be smooth.
4. Hands, wrists and arms should look natural and feel soft and relaxed.
5. All flams should have the same quality of sound.

8. Chromatic Exercises in Fifths

8-1 Moving Down and Up

ⓜ = Muffle (dampen)
*Xylophone, Bells, Marimba, Vibes
𝄂𝄐 (Vibes only)

Percussion Goals
1. Breathe together and start together.
2. Posture should be natural with the body position balanced.
3. Match the dynamic level of the winds.
4. Triangle and tambourine each should have a consistent quality of sound, note-to-note.
5. All flams should have the same quality of sound.

8-2 Moving Up and Down

 Percussion Goals
1. Breathe together and start together.
2. Posture should be natural with the body position balanced.
3. Match the dynamic level of the winds.
4. Triangle and tambourine each should have a consistent quality of sound, note-to-note.
5. All flams should have the same quality of sound.

9. Rhythm and Tonguing Exercises with Triplets

9-1 Long to Short Notes

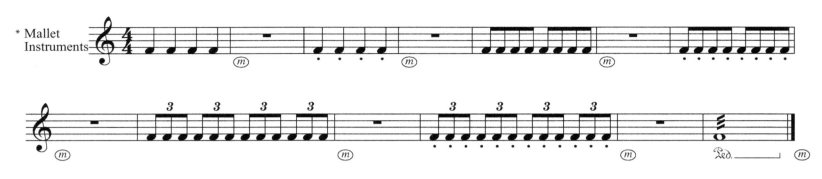

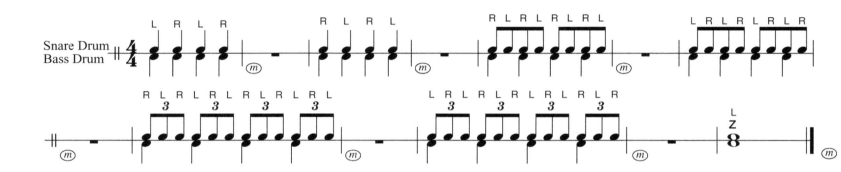

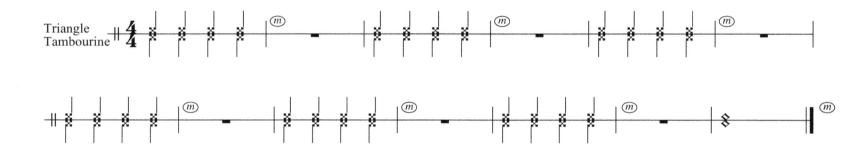

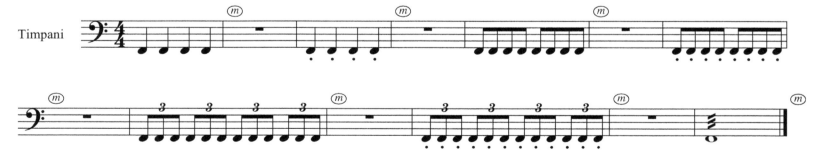

 = Muffle (dampen)

*Xylophone, Bells, Marimba, Vibes

Ped. (Vibes only)

Percussion Goals

1. Breathe together and start together.
2. Dampen to match the end of the wind players' notes.
3. Match the dynamic level of the winds.
4. Strike the instrument in the same place with the same energy every time.
5. The hand, wrist and arm motion should look the same hand-to-hand.

9-2 Short to Long Notes

Percussion Goals
1. Breathe together and start together.
2. Dampen to match the end of the wind players' notes.
3. Match the dynamic level of the winds.
4. Strike the instrument in the same place with the same energy every time.
5. The hand, wrist and arm motion should look the same hand-to-hand.

10. Combining Eighth and Sixteenth Notes

Variation 1

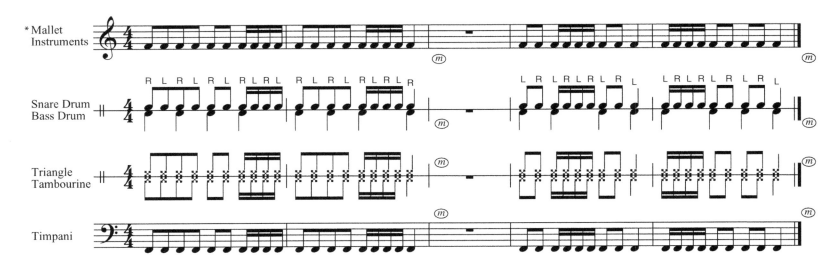

Variation 2

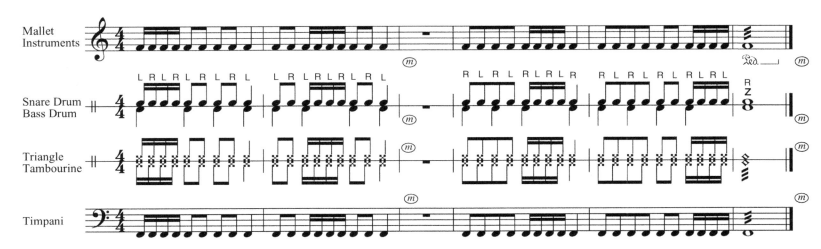

Variation 3

ⓜ = Muffle (dampen)
*Xylophone, Bells, Marimba, Vibes
🎵 (Vibes only)

Percussion Goals for Variations 1-3

1. Breathe together and start together.
2. The quicker the notes, the smoother the mallet/stick motion should look.
3. Rolls should be smooth and even.
4. Strike the instrument in the same place with the same energy every time.
5. Posture should be natural with the body position balanced.

Variation 4

Variation 5

Variation 6

 Percussion Goals for Variations 4-6

1. Breathe together and start together.
2. The quicker the notes, the smoother the mallet/stick motion should look.
3. Rolls should be smooth and even.
4. Strike the instrument in the same place with the same energy every time.
5. Posture should be natural with the body position balanced.